Our Favorite
Christmas recipes

Copyright 2008, Gooseberry Patch
Third Printing, September, 2012

Cover: Candy Cane Thumbprints (page 111)

Single servings...roll your Holiday Cheese Ball into mini balls and place in paper muffin cups. Fill more muffin cups with crackers and pretzels and arrange alongside mini cheese balls...guests can enjoy one of each!

Holiday Cheese Ball

Makes one cheese ball

1 t. onion juice
1 t. Worcestershire sauce
1/2 c. fresh parsley, chopped
8-oz. pkg. cream cheese
1/2-lb. sharp Cheddar cheese,
    grated

4-oz. pkg. crumbled blue cheese
3/4 c. chopped pecans, divided
Garnish: pecans and fresh
    parsley

Combine first 6 ingredients together in a mixing bowl, stir in 1/2 cup pecans and shape into a ball. Roll cheese ball in 1/4 cup of pecans. Garnish with whole pecans and fresh parsley. Let stand at room temperature for one hour before serving.

Fill baskets with dippers like pretzels, bagel chips,
veggies and potato chips. Set an inverted plate or shallow
pan under one side of the bottom of each basket to create
a tilt...it looks so nice and guests can grab dippers easily!

Sweet Pumpkin Dip

Makes about 9 cups

2 8-oz. pkgs. cream cheese,
   softened
4 c. powdered sugar
30-oz. can pumpkin pie
   filling mix

2 t. cinnamon
1 t. ground ginger
gingersnap cookies

Mix cream cheese and powdered sugar in a large bowl. Blend in pie filling and spices; cover and chill. Serve with gingersnaps for dipping.

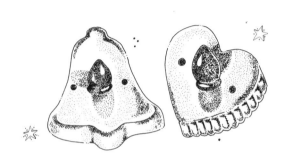

Use mini cookie cutters to cut toasted bread into holiday shapes to serve alongside savory dips and spreads.

Parmesan-Bacon Dip

Makes about 3 cups

2 8-oz. pkgs. cream cheese, softened
1/3 c. grated Parmesan cheese
1/3 c. green pepper, diced
1/2 c. green onion, chopped

1/2 c. mayonnaise-type salad dressing
10 slices bacon, crisply cooked and crumbled

In a medium mixing bowl, blend together all ingredients; chill before serving.

Quickly dress up a table by filling a glass bowl with seasonal objects like pine cones and ornaments.

Christmas Cheddar Wafers

Makes 6 dozen

8-oz. pkg. shredded sharp
    Cheddar cheese
1 c. all-purpose flour
1/2 c. butter, softened

1/2 t. seasoned salt
1/8 t. cayenne pepper
1/2 c. chopped pecans

Mix all ingredients, then form into a roll one-inch in diameter;
wrap in wax paper and chill for about one hour. Slice 1/4-inch thick
and bake on ungreased baking sheets at 350 degrees for 10 to
12 minutes.

For stand-up parties, make it easy for guests by serving foods that can be eaten in just one or 2 bites.

Mini Ham Puffs

Makes 2 dozen

1/4 lb. cooked ham, finely
    chopped
1 onion, finely chopped
1/2 c. shredded Swiss cheese
1 egg, beaten

1-1/2 t. Dijon mustard
1/8 t. pepper
8-oz. tube refrigerated crescent
    rolls

Place ham and onion in mixing bowl. Add cheese, egg, mustard and
pepper; mix well. Lightly spray muffin pan with non-stick spray. Unroll
crescent rolls and press dough into large rectangle. Cut rectangle into
24 pieces using pizza cutter. Press dough pieces into muffin cups.
Fill each muffin cup with ham filling. Bake at 350 degrees for
13 to 15 minutes or until golden brown.

A good rule of thumb when serving appetizers is 6 to 8 per person if dinner will follow, and 12 to 15 per person if it's an appetizer-only gathering.

Cherry Tomato Appetizers

Makes 2 dozen

1 pt. cherry tomatoes
salt to taste
8 slices bacon, crisply cooked
    and crumbled

1/2 c. mayonnaise
1 shallot, finely chopped
Garnish: fresh parsley

Cut a thin slice off the round end of each tomato; tomatoes will sit on the stem end. Using a small sharp knife or a melon ball scoop, remove the seeds and juice from the center of each tomato, leaving the shell. Salt the inside of tomato shells and drain upside down on a paper towel for at least 1/2 hour or overnight in the refrigerator. Mix bacon, mayonnaise and shallot. Using a small spoon, stuff each tomato with mayonnaise mixture. Garnish with parsley.

Add pizzazz to an appetizer tray...glue tiny Christmas balls
onto long toothpicks for serving.

Festive Holiday Spread   *Makes 10 to 12 servings*

8-oz. pkg. cream cheese,
   softened
4-oz. can chopped black olives,
   drained
4-1/2 oz. can chopped green
   chiles

1 bunch green onions, chopped
16-oz. container sour cream
1 tomato, chopped

Blend together cream cheese, olives, chiles and onions. Place spread on a serving platter and form into a candy cane shape. Cover with plastic wrap and chill; remove 15 minutes before serving. Spread sour cream over spread. Sprinkle tomatoes over sour cream to form stripes. Serve with assorted crackers.

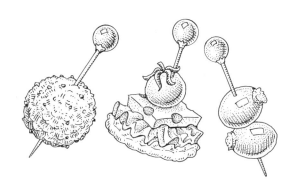

Quick & easy appetizers...wrap pear slices with prosciutto
or melon wedges with thinly-sliced turkey. Ready in a snap!

Christmas Puffs

Makes 2-1/2 dozen

3 T. butter, melted
1 t. dried, minced onion

10-oz. tube refrigerated biscuits
1/4 c. grated Parmesan cheese

Spread butter in a 9"x9" baking pan and sprinkle with onion. Cut each biscuit into 4 pieces; arrange in dish and sprinkle with Parmesan. Bake at 425 degrees for 15 minutes, until golden.

Use pretty glass trifle bowls to hold pillar candles.
Keep them in place with glittery sugar or cranberries.

Wintry Snack Mix

Makes 10 cups

1 c. semi-sweet chocolate chips
1/2 c. creamy peanut butter
1/4 c. butter
1 t. vanilla extract

9 c. bite-size crispy cereal
   squares
1-1/2 c. powdered sugar

Combine chocolate chips, peanut butter and butter in a microwave-safe bowl and microwave on high, uncovered, for one minute. Stir; microwave an additional 30 seconds, and stir again until smooth. Blend in vanilla. Place cereal in a large bowl; pour mixture over cereal, stirring until cereal is coated. Spoon into a large plastic zipping bag, add powdered sugar, and shake until well coated. Store in an airtight container.

May our house always be too small to hold all of our friends.

—Myrtle Reed

Parmesan Crostini

Makes one dozen

1 baguette loaf, sliced into
   12 rounds

1 to 2 T. olive oil
1/4 c. grated Parmesan cheese

Brush baguette slices lightly with olive oil. Arrange slices on an ungreased baking sheet; sprinkle one teaspoon cheese on each. Place baking sheet under broiler, about 6 inches from heat, for one to 2 minutes, until cheese begins to melt. Makes one dozen.

Keep beverages warm and always have a napkin handy...
wrap them together. Just wrap a napkin around a mug
and secure with a napkin ring. Fill the mug with
Christmas Wassail...quick & easy!

Christmas Wassail

Makes 3 quarts

1 qt. water
1-1/2 c. sugar
5 4-inch cinnamon sticks
10 whole cloves
5 thin slices fresh ginger root

2 c. strong brewed tea
1 qt. cider
6-oz. can frozen orange juice
    concentrate, thawed
2 T. lemon juice

Combine water and sugar in a large saucepan; heat over low heat until sugar is dissolved. Add cinnamon, cloves and ginger and let simmer on low for 2 hours, or turn off heat and set aside overnight. Remove spices with a slotted spoon; add tea, cider, orange juice and lemon juice. Heat and serve warm.

Wrap a length of wired, sparkly beads around the stems of glasses...a whimsical beverage marker!

Peppermint Eggnog Punch

Makes 16 servings

1 qt. peppermint ice cream,
    divided
1 qt. eggnog

Optional: 1 c. rum
4 12-oz. cans ginger ale, chilled
Garnish: 24 mini candy canes

Set aside 2 or 3 scoops ice cream for garnish; freeze. Soften remaining ice cream; gradually stir in eggnog and rum, if using. Transfer to a punch bowl and pour in ginger ale. Garnish edge of punch bowl with candy canes. Float reserved ice cream scoops on top; serve immediately.

A punch bowl is a festive touch that makes even the simplest
party beverage special! Surround it with a wreath of
pine cones and greenery.

Apple-Cinnamon Punch

Makes 25 cups

1 c. water
1/2 c. sugar
1/2 c. red cinnamon candies

2 2-ltr. bottles raspberry ginger ale, chilled
46-oz. can apple juice, chilled

Combine water, sugar and candies in a small saucepan; bring to a boil. Reduce heat and simmer, uncovered, for 5 minutes or until candies melt; stir occasionally. When mixture has cooled, combine with ginger ale and apple juice; stir well.

Bring out the slow cooker for your party. Guests will
follow the fragrance of a warm drink coming from the crock.
Leave beverages on low setting during the gathering and guests
can just ladle their drinks right from the cooker.

Mama's Warm Spiced Milk

Makes 4 servings

2-1/2 c. milk
1/3 c. apple butter
2-1/2 T. maple syrup
1/4 t. cinnamon

1/8 t. ground cloves
Garnish: vanilla powder,
     4-inch cinnamon sticks

Whisk ingredients together, except garnish, in a heavy medium saucepan. Heat over low heat until milk steams (do not boil). Serve sprinkled with vanilla powder and a cinnamon stick for stirring.

Fruit butter is yummy spread on dinner rolls. Combine 1/2 cup softened butter with one cup powdered sugar and one to 2 cups sliced berries or fruit. Place in a food processor and process until smooth. Refrigerate and use within one week.

Rosebud Dinner Rolls

Makes 2 dozen

1 c. lukewarm water
1 env. active dry yeast
2 c. milk
1/2 c. sugar

1/2 c. butter, melted
1 T. salt
3 eggs, beaten
5 c. all-purpose flour, divided

Heat water to between 110 and 115 degrees; add yeast, stir to dissolve. Heat milk in a medium saucepan just to boiling; set aside to cool. Stir sugar, butter and salt into milk; add to yeast mixture. By hand, or using a heavy-duty mixer, beat eggs and 3 cups flour into yeast mixture. Add enough remaining flour to form a stiff dough. To prepare rosebud rolls, divide dough in half and roll into 2 ropes. Divide each rope into 12 equal pieces and shape each piece into a ball. Place balls 3 inches apart on a greased baking sheet. Let rise until almost double. Begin at the center of each roll and use a knife to make 5 cuts in the rolls. Bake at 350 degrees for 25 to 30 minutes.

Run a bead of hot glue along the sides of tealights and decorate with ribbon, beads, or hard candies. Arrange on a pedestal plate for a centerpiece...the centerpiece is done!

Poppy Seed Bread

Makes 2 loaves

2-1/2 c. sugar
1-1/2 t. baking powder
2 T. poppy seeds
3 c. all-purpose flour
1 t. salt
2 c. milk, divided

2 t. vanilla extract, divided
1-1/2 t. almond extract
1 c. oil
3 eggs, beaten
1 c. powdered sugar

Stir together first 5 ingredients in large mixing bowl. Add 1-1/2 cups milk, 1-1/2 teaspoons vanilla, almond extract, oil and eggs. Beat on medium speed for 2 minutes. Pour into 2 greased and floured 9"x5" loaf pans. Bake in a 350 degree oven for 50 to 55 minutes. Mix remaining milk, vanilla and powdered sugar together until smooth. While bread is still warm, brush with glaze. Allow to cool in pans.

Layer slices of holiday quick breads in berry baskets...
top with a rick rack bow.

Quick Holiday Loaf

Makes one loaf

1/2 c. currants
1/2 c. red and green candied
    cherries, chopped
1/2 c. dried pears, chopped
1/2 c. chopped walnuts
1 c. applesauce
1 c. sugar

2 eggs, beaten
1/2 c. oil
2 t. lemon zest
1-1/2 t. baking powder
1/2 t. baking soda
1/2 t. salt
2-1/4 c. all-purpose flour

Combine first 4 ingredients in a bowl; stir to mix. Reserve 1/2 cup for topping; set aside remaining mixture. Mix applesauce and sugar until sugar dissolves; beat in eggs, oil, lemon zest, baking powder, baking soda and salt until well blended. Stir in flour and fruit mixture; spread evenly into a greased 9"x5" loaf pan. Sprinkle with reserved fruit mixture. Bake at 325 degrees for one hour and 10 minutes, or until a knife tip comes out with moist crumbs attached. Cool in pan 10 minutes; run a knife around edges and invert onto a wire rack to cool completely.

Children's woolen mittens or stockings are darling
on a tiny greenery wreath.

Eggnog Bread

Makes one loaf

2-1/4 c. all-purpose flour
3/4 c. sugar
1 T. baking powder
1 t. salt
1/2 t. nutmeg
1-1/2 c. eggnog

1/4 c. butter, melted
1 egg, beaten
1/2 c. dried apricots, chopped
1/2 c. dried cherries
3/4 c. pecans, chopped

Sift together flour, sugar, baking powder, salt and nutmeg; set aside. In a separate bowl, blend together eggnog, butter and egg. Mix with dry ingredients, stirring until just blended. Fold in apricots, cherries and pecans. Spread batter in a lightly oiled and floured 9"x5" loaf pan. Bake at 350 degrees for 50 minutes to one hour, or until bread tests done. Remove loaf from pan and cool on wire rack.

Sprinkle powdered sugar or cocoa through a doily
for a pretty yet simple cake decoration...check craft stores
for holiday stencils too!

Date-Nut-Cherry Fruitcake

Makes 2 loaves

1-1/2 c. all-purpose flour
1-1/2 c. sugar
1 t. baking powder
1 t. salt
16-oz. pkg. chopped dates

16-oz. pkg. chopped walnuts
16-oz. jar maraschino cherries,
    drained
5 eggs, beaten
1 t. vanilla extract

Combine flour, sugar, baking powder and salt; stir in dates, walnuts
and cherries. Set aside. Beat eggs and vanilla together; add to flour
mixture. Pour into 2 greased 9"x5" loaf pans; bake at 325 degrees
for one hour.

Slip cranberries onto lengths of florist's wire and then shape them
into stars...so pretty hanging in each of your windowpanes!

40

Cornbread Stuffing

Makes 16 servings

16-oz. pkg. cornbread
    stuffing mix
3 c. water
1/2 c. butter, divided
1 c. onion, chopped
1 c. celery, chopped

1 c. ground Italian sausage,
    browned and drained
1 c. sweetened, dried
    cranberries
1/2 c. chopped pecans

Prepare stuffing according to package directions using 3 cups water
and 1/4 cup butter; set aside. Sauté the onion and celery in remaining
butter until translucent. Stir onion, celery, sausage, cranberries and
pecans into stuffing; toss well to coat. Spread in a lightly greased
13"x9" baking pan; bake at 350 degrees for 30 minutes.

A shimmering welcome...set tealights inside frosted juice
glasses. So pretty on porch steps or along a walkway.

Crockery Sage Dressing

Makes 10 to 12 servings

2 c. onion, chopped
2 c. celery, chopped
1 c. butter
2 loaves white bread, torn
1-1/2 t. dried sage
1 t. dried thyme

1/2 t. dried marjoram
1 t. poultry seasoning
1-1/2 t. salt
1/2 t. pepper
15-oz. can chicken broth
2 eggs, beaten

Sauté onion and celery in butter in a medium skillet; set aside. Place bread in a large mixing bowl; add seasonings and toss well. Add onion mixture and enough broth to moisten bread; toss well. Stir in eggs and mix well. Spoon into a slow cooker. Cook on low setting for 4 to 6 hours, stirring occasionally and adding more broth as needed.

Bells are magical...wire different sizes on a wreath or string
several on ribbon and hang from a doorknob.

Apple-Mallow Yam Bake

Makes 6 to 8 servings

2 apples, cored and sliced
1/3 c. chopped pecans
1/2 c. brown sugar, packed
1/2 t. cinnamon

2 17-oz. cans sweet potatoes,
    drained and sliced
1/4 c. margarine, diced
2 c. mini marshmallows

Toss apples and nuts with brown sugar and cinnamon. Alternate layers of apple mixture and sweet potatoes in a greased 1-1/2 quart casserole dish; dot with margarine. Cover and bake at 350 degrees for 35 to 40 minutes. Sprinkle marshmallows on top and broil until golden.

No mantel for hanging stockings? Mount Shaker pegs
on a wooden board, one for each member of the family!

Sweet Potato Casserole

Makes 8 servings

1 c. all-purpose flour
2/3 c. brown sugar, packed
1/4 c. chopped pecans, toasted
1/4 c. margarine
1/2 t. cinnamon
4 sweet potatoes, peeled and
   halved

1/2 c. sugar
1-1/2 t. vanilla extract
1 egg white, beaten
5-oz. can fat-free evaporated
   milk

Combine first 5 ingredients in a small bowl, stirring until mixture resembles coarse crumbs; set aside. Place potatoes in a Dutch oven; add water to cover. Bring to a boil, cover and reduce heat. Simmer 30 minutes or until potatoes are very tender; drain well. Mash potatoes in a large bowl. Stir in one cup pecan mixture, sugar, vanilla, egg white and milk. Spoon into a 2-quart casserole dish coated with non-stick vegetable spray; top with remaining pecan mixture. Bake, uncovered, at 350 degrees for 45 minutes.

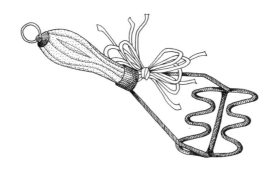

Roll balls of leftover mashed potatoes in a mixture
of Parmesan cheese and seasoned bread crumbs...
broil until golden. Delicious!

Garlic Mashed Potatoes

Makes 8 servings

2 to 4 cloves garlic
2 T. plus 1 t. butter, divided
1 t. olive oil
5 potatoes, peeled and chopped
2 t. salt

1/4 c. sour cream
1/2 c. warm milk
1/4 c. fresh chives, snipped
salt and pepper to taste

To roast garlic, peel each clove and place in a one-pint oven-proof baker. Add one teaspoon butter and olive oil. Bake, covered, at 325 degrees for 45 minutes. The cloves should be golden, but not brown. Remove from oven, cool slightly, then mash with a fork; set aside. In 4-1/2 quart saucepan add potatoes and enough water to cover. Stir in salt and bring to a boil. Reduce heat to a simmer and continue to cook until tender, about 15 to 20 minutes. Drain; beat with an electric mixer on medium speed. Add remaining butter and continue to beat until well blended. Add sour cream, milk, chives, garlic and season to taste.

Tie ornaments onto the Christmas tree with narrow strips of homespun fabric...sweet and simple!

Cheddar Potatoes

Makes 8 to 10 servings

8 to 10 potatoes, peeled and chopped

8-oz. pkg. cream cheese, softened

1-oz. pkg. ranch salad dressing mix

2 c. shredded Cheddar cheese

Cover potatoes with water, bring to a boil and cook until tender. Drain; add cream cheese and ranch mix. Beat with a mixer on medium speed until potatoes are fluffy. Place in a 2-quart casserole dish, sprinkle with Cheddar cheese and bake, uncovered, at 350 degrees for 20 minutes.

For a warm glow at dinner, place a floating candle in
a water-filled wine glass at each place setting.

Creamed Peas & Onions

Makes 4 to 6 servings

4 T. butter
4 T. all-purpose flour
1-1/2 c. milk
16-oz. pkg. frozen peas and
    onions, thawed

1 t. onion powder
salt and pepper to taste

Melt butter in a large skillet over low heat; blend in flour until smooth. Increase heat to medium and add milk, 1/2 cup at a time, until thickened. Stir in peas and onions; add onion powder, salt and pepper. Heat through.

For a magical centerpiece, create a winter wonderland
on a cake pedestal using miniature trees and sugar for snow.
A clear dome keeps it beautiful!

Savory Spinach

Makes 8 to 10 servings

3 10-oz. pkgs. frozen chopped
   spinach, cooked and
   drained

8-oz. container sour cream
1-1/2 oz. pkg. onion soup mix

Mix together all ingredients; spoon into a greased 2-quart casserole
dish. Bake, covered, at 350 degrees for 30 minutes.

Get a head start on your holiday open house. Bundle up silverware in cloth napkins a few days in advance and place in a festive basket. They'll be ready to go to the table when you are!

Cheesy Scalloped Corn

Makes 8 to 10 servings

2 eggs, slightly beaten
11-oz. can corn, drained, liquid
    reserved
14-3/4 oz. can creamed corn
5-oz. can evaporated milk
4 T. butter, melted

2 T. dried, minced onion
1/8 t. salt
1/8 t. pepper
2 c. saltine crackers, coarsely
    crushed
8-oz. pkg. Swiss cheese, diced

Combine eggs, corn and 1/2 cup reserved corn liquid in a large bowl;
add cream-style corn, milk, butter, onion, salt and pepper. Lightly stir
in saltines and cheese. Spray an 8"x8" casserole dish with non-stick
vegetable spray. Pour in mixture and bake, covered, at 350 degrees
for 50 minutes. Uncover and bake an additional 10 minutes until set.
Let stand for 5 minutes before serving.

Add big red ribbon bows to stair railings, drawer handles, lamp bases and potted plants for a dash of Christmas color in a snap.

Old-Fashioned Corn Pudding

Makes 4 to 6 servings

2 eggs, beaten
1/4 to 1/2 c. sugar
2 slices bread, crusts trimmed

14-3/4 oz. can creamed corn
1/2 c. evaporated milk
1 t. vanilla extract

Mix together eggs and sugar; cube bread and add to mixture. Stir in corn, milk and vanilla. Pour mixture into a buttered 1-1/2 quart casserole dish. Bake, uncovered, at 350 degrees for one hour.

Turn a toboggan into a clever wintertime serving table!
Just set it securely on top of a buffet table, toss on a plaid
throw, and then load it up with lots of salads, sides and breads.

Spiced Fruit

Makes 6 to 8 servings

29-oz. can sliced peaches
15-1/4 oz. can apricot halves
3/4 c. brown sugar, packed
1/2 c. white vinegar
4 4-inch cinnamon sticks

1 t. whole cloves
1 T. whole allspice
20-oz. can pineapple chunks,
    drained

Drain the juice from the peaches and apricots into a large saucepan;
add brown sugar, vinegar, cinnamon sticks, cloves and allspice. Bring
to a boil and boil for 5 minutes. Add pineapple chunks, peaches and
apricots to the saucepan; reduce heat and simmer until fruit is warm.
Remove cinnamon sticks and cloves.

A wide satin ribbon draped over the back of each chair
makes a quick-as-a-wink placecard. Just rubber stamp
the guest's name on each ribbon.

Herbed Rice Pilaf

Makes 8 servings

1/4 c. butter
2 c. long-grain rice, uncooked
1 c. celery, chopped
1/2 c. onion, chopped
4 c. chicken broth

1 t. Worcestershire sauce
1 t. soy sauce
1 t. dried oregano
1 t. dried thyme

Melt butter in a saucepan, stir in rice, celery and onion. Sauté until rice is lightly browned and the celery and onion become tender. Transfer to a lightly oiled 2-quart casserole dish. Whisk together remaining ingredients and pour over rice mixture. Bake, covered, at 325 degrees for 50 minutes or until rice is tender.

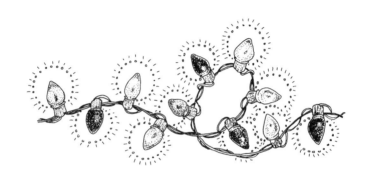

Add a warm glow to the party with a simple strand of lights.
Decorate the table with a string of white lights folded inside a
sheer table runner or strip of fabric. Sparkly!

Christmas Eve Pot Roast

Makes 6 to 8 servings

2 t. salt
1/2 t. pepper
1 t. paprika
1 t. garlic powder
4 to 5-lb. boneless chuck roast
3 T. all-purpose flour
2 T. oil
2/3 c. water

2 bay leaves
3 onions, quartered
5 carrots, peeled and quartered
4 potatoes, peeled and quartered
14-1/2 oz. can Italian-style
    diced tomatoes with juice
15-oz. can tomato sauce

Blend seasonings in a small bowl; rub into roast and coat with flour.
Heat oil in a heavy saucepan or Dutch oven; add roast and brown
briefly on all sides over high heat. Add water and bay leaves to pan;
cover, reduce heat to low and simmer for 2 hours. Add remaining
ingredients, cover and simmer for an additional hour. Remove and
discard bay leaves.

Pull out vintage finds when setting a buffet table. An old door hinge becomes a clever napkin holder when a sprig of greenery is tied on. Its weight keeps napkins in their place...how clever!

Perfect Prime Rib Roast

Makes 6 to 8 servings

1/4 c. Worcestershire sauce
2 t. garlic powder
2 t. seasoned salt

2 t. pepper
6-lb. bone-in beef rib roast

In a small bowl, combine first four ingredients. Rub mixture over roast; place in a large plastic zipping bag. Refrigerate 8 hours or overnight, turning often. Place roast fat-side up in a lightly greased large roasting pan; pour mixture from bag over roast. Cover with aluminum foil; bake at 350 degrees for 1-1/2 hours. Uncover and bake for an additional 1-1/2 hours, or until roast reaches desired temperature on a meat thermometer, between 150 and 160 degrees for medium. Let stand for 15 minutes before slicing.

Apply adhesive-backed gold stars onto plain pillar candles
for quick holiday decorations.

Maple-Glazed Turkey Breast

Makes 4 servings

6-oz. pkg. long-grain and
    wild rice mix, uncooked
1-1/4 c. water
1-lb. turkey breast

1/4 c. maple syrup
1/2 c. chopped walnuts
1/2 t. cinnamon

Mix together rice, seasoning packet from rice mix and water in a slow cooker. Place turkey breast, skin-side up, on rice mixture. Drizzle with syrup; sprinkle with walnuts and cinnamon. Cover and cook on low setting 4 to 5 hours, or until juices run clear when turkey breast is pierced with a fork.

Stack ribbon-tied bundles of sweetly scented candles
in a basket near the front door...a pretty decoration
that doubles as gifts for surprise visitors.

Easy Elegant Turkey

Makes 10 to 15 servings

14-lb. turkey, thawed
salt and pepper to taste
1 stalk celery, chopped
1 onion, chopped

12 bay leaves
6 sprigs fresh parsley
1/2 c. butter, melted

Pat turkey dry with paper towels. Remove giblets and neck; season cavity with salt and pepper. Place celery and onion in cavity. Gently lift skin of turkey breast by inserting fingers under skin. Insert bay leaves and parsley springs. Pull skin back down over turkey. Line a large roasting pan with aluminum foil, leaving enough foil over the sides to cover turkey. Place turkey in roasting pan; pour melted butter over top and salt and pepper to taste. Loosely cover turkey with foil. Bake at 450 degrees for 2-1/2 to 2-3/4 hours, or until a meat thermometer inserted into the thickest part of the inner thigh registers 180 degrees. Remove foil during last hour of baking to brown. Let turkey rest 15 minutes before transferring to a serving platter to slice.

Clip mini round glass ornaments around the bottom rim of
a lampshade...a sparkling touch for the holidays.

Holiday Roast Turkey

Makes 10 to 12 servings

14 to 15-lb. turkey, thawed
2 cloves garlic, halved and
    divided
1 t. seasoning salt, divided
1 onion, quartered

1 bunch fresh parsley
2 fresh thyme sprigs
5 to 6 leaves fresh sage
2 T. olive oil
pepper to taste

Rinse turkey and pat dry. Remove giblets and neck; reserve for another use. Rub inside of turkey with one clove garlic and 1/2 teaspoon salt; stuff with remaining garlic, onion and herbs. Place turkey breast-side up on a rack in a large roaster pan. Brush oil over turkey; sprinkle with remaining salt and pepper to taste. Roast turkey at 325 degrees about 2-3/4 to 3 hours, basting occasionally with pan drippings, until a meat thermometer inserted into thickest part of thigh registers 180 degrees. If needed, tent turkey with aluminum foil to prevent browning too quickly. Let turkey stand 15 to 20 minutes before carving; discard garlic, onion and herbs.

Bake up a quiche with leftover ham, chopped veggies and cheese.
Put about a cup of ingredients in a pie crust, then whisk together
3 eggs and a small can of evaporated milk. Pour into crust and
bake at 400 degrees until set, 20 to 25 minutes. Scrumptious!

Whole Baked Ham

Makes 18 to 20 servings

12 to 14-lb. fully cooked
   boneless or semi-boneless
   ham
12 whole cloves
1-1/2 c. pineapple juice

1/2 c. maple syrup
6 slices canned pineapple
1 c. water
3/4 c. brown sugar, packed
3 T. mustard

Place ham, fat side up, in a shallow roasting pan. Press cloves into top of ham. Stir together pineapple juice and syrup; pour over ham. Arrange pineapple slices on ham, secure with toothpicks. Bake at 325 degrees for 1-1/2 hours. Add water and bake for 1-1/2 additional hours. Remove from oven; discard pineapple slices. Mix together brown sugar and mustard; spread over ham. Bake an additional 30 minutes.

A fragrant, spicy table accent...press whole cloves into the
surface of a pillar candle to form a pattern.

Cranberry-Glazed Pork Roast   *Makes 12 servings*

2 t. cornstarch
1/4 t. cinnamon
1/8 t. salt
1/2 t. orange zest

2 T. orange juice
16 oz. whole-berry cranberry
    sauce
4-lb. boneless pork loin roast

In a small saucepan, stir together all ingredients except pork. Cook, stirring over medium heat until thickened; set aside. Place roast in shallow baking dish. Roast at 325 degrees for 45 minutes. Spoon 1/2 cup glaze over roast and continue roasting for 30 to 45 minutes or until meat thermometer reads 155 to 160 degrees. Let stand 10 minutes before slicing and serve with remaining sauce.

A hollowed-out round loaf of bread is terrific for holding
dinner rolls or salads. If no one nibbles on it after it's empty,
share it as a Christmas treat for the birds!

Cider-Baked Ham

Makes 18 to 20 servings

12 to 14-lb. cooked ham
2 c. apple cider
4-inch cinnamon stick
1 t. whole cloves

1/2 t. allspice
1/2 c. brown sugar, packed
1/2 c. honey
Garnish: whole cloves

Place ham in a shallow roasting pan. Combine apple cider, cinnamon stick, cloves and allspice in a small saucepan; heat to boiling. Cover and simmer for 5 minutes; pour over ham. Bake, uncovered, at 325 degrees, basting every 30 minutes with cider sauce for about 3 hours. Remove ham from oven. Increase oven temperature to 400 degrees. Score diagonal lines in fat with the tip of a knife to form diamond shapes, being careful not to cut into meat. Stud each diamond with a whole clove. Combine brown sugar and honey in a small saucepan. Cook over low heat, stirring until sugar is melted. Brush over top of ham. Return ham to 400 degree oven. Bake 30 additional minutes, brushing ham every 10 minutes with remaining honey mixture until meat thermometer registers 160 degrees. Remove from oven. Let stand 20 minutes before slicing.

March a set of colorful wooden nutcrackers up the stairs...
a sweet, nostalgic greeting!

Italian Stuffed Chicken

Makes 4 servings

1 c. sliced mushrooms
2 T. butter
1 c. ricotta cheese
1 c. shredded mozzarella cheese
1/2 c. grated Parmesan cheese

1/2 c. dried parsley
1/4 c. Italian-seasoned dry
    bread crumbs
4 chicken breasts
paprika to taste

In a skillet over medium heat, sauté mushrooms in butter until tender; set aside. Combine cheeses, parsley and bread crumbs; mix well. Stir in mushroom mixture. With your fingers, separate skin from chicken breasts. Spoon mixture underneath skin; sprinkle with paprika. Arrange chicken in a lightly greased 13"x9" baking pan. Bake, uncovered, at 350 degrees for 30 minutes, or until juice runs clear.

Shop flea markets for all kinds of cookie cutters...they make
terrific ornaments, package tie-on's and napkin rings.

Busy-Day Lasagna

Makes 6 to 8 servings

12-oz. container cottage cheese
4 c. shredded mozzarella
    cheese, divided
2 eggs, beaten
1/3 c. grated Parmesan cheese
1/3 c. dried parsley
1 t. onion powder

1/2 t. dried basil
1/8 t. pepper
32-oz. jar spaghetti sauce
1 lb. ground beef, browned and
    drained
9 lasagna noodles, uncooked
1/4 c. water

Mix together cottage cheese, 2 cups mozzarella cheese, eggs, Parmesan cheese and seasonings; set aside. Combine spaghetti sauce and beef; set aside. Spread one to 1-1/2 cups of meat mixture into an ungreased 13"x9" baking pan; layer 5 lasagna noodles, half the cottage cheese mixture and 1-1/2 cups of meat mixture. Add remaining layer of lasagna; cover with remaining meat mixture. Top with remaining mozzarella cheese; pour water around the edges. Bake, covered, at 350 degrees for 45 minutes; uncover and bake for an additional 15 minutes.

Fill straight-sided hurricanes with bright red and green
shiny apples or fresh pears to decorate your holiday
dinner table. It's a natural!

3-Cheese Shells Florentine

Makes 6 servings

10-oz. pkg. frozen chopped
   spinach, thawed and drained
1-3/4 c. cottage cheese
1 egg, beaten
1/4 c. grated Parmesan cheese
1 c. shredded mozzarella
   cheese, divided

1/3 c. fresh parsley, chopped
salt and pepper to taste
7-oz. pkg. small shell macaroni,
   cooked
1-1/2 to 2 16-oz. jars Alfredo
   sauce, divided

Combine spinach, cottage cheese, egg, Parmesan cheese, 2/3 cup
mozzarella, parsley, salt and pepper in a large mixing bowl. Set
aside. In another bowl, toss macaroni with 2-1/2 cups Alfredo sauce.
Arrange half of macaroni in a lightly greased 13"x9" baking pan.
Layer spinach mixture evenly over macaroni. Cover with remaining
macaroni, Alfredo sauce and remaining mozzarella, in that order.
Bake, uncovered, at 350 degrees for 35 to 40 minutes.

Turn tissue paper into festive filler for gift baskets in a wink...
just run it through a paper shredder!

Triple Chocolate Bundt® Cake

Makes 10 servings

18-1/4 oz. pkg. devil's food
    cake mix
4-1/2 oz. pkg. instant chocolate
    pudding mix
1-3/4 c. milk

12-oz. pkg. semi-sweet
    chocolate chips
2 eggs, beaten
Garnish: powdered sugar

Combine cake mix, pudding mix, milk, chocolate chips and eggs in a
large bowl. Mix until well blended, about 2 minutes. Pour batter into
a greased and floured Bundt® pan. Bake at 350 degrees for 50 to
55 minutes, until cake springs back when touched. Do not over bake.
Turn out onto a serving plate; sprinkle powdered sugar over top
before serving.

Make holiday cookies and candy look magical. Sprinkle on edible glitter, confetti and colorful sugar...so festive!

Peppermint Snowballs

Makes 2-1/2 dozen

18-oz. pkg. chocolate sandwich
   cookies, finely crushed
8-oz. pkg. cream cheese,
   softened

6-oz. pkg. white melting
   chocolate
1 to 1-1/2 c. peppermint
   candies, finely crushed

Mix together crushed cookies and cream cheese. Roll into 1-1/2 inch balls and set aside. Melt white chocolate in the top of a double boiler over low heat; stir in crushed candy. Dip balls into chocolate and set on wax paper to harden.

Ever had Sugar-on-Snow? Gather a pail of freshly fallen snow.
Spoon it into serving bowls and top with warm maple syrup.
A wonderful New England wintertime treat!

Baked Cinnamon Pudding

Makes 12 servings

2 c. brown sugar, packed
1-1/2 c. cold water
4 T. butter, divided
1 c. sugar
1 c. milk

1-2/3 c. all-purpose flour
2 t. baking powder
2 t. cinnamon
1/2 c. chopped nuts

Blend together brown sugar, water and 2 tablespoons butter in a saucepan. Bring to a boil; set aside. Combine sugar, remaining butter, milk, flour, baking powder and cinnamon; place in the bottom of an ungreased 13"x9" baking dish. Pour brown sugar mixture over top and sprinkle with nuts. Bake at 350 degrees for 45 minutes.

Nestle mini cookies or fudge inside a pretty teacup and give
with a box of herbal tea...a warming go-with for
your cookie treats.

Snowy Day Fudge

Makes about 5 dozen

14-oz. can sweetened
   condensed milk
1-1/2 c. white chocolate chips

1/2 c. butterscotch chips
1/2 c. peanut butter chips
1/2 c. milk chocolate chips

Combine all ingredients in a heavy saucepan over medium heat.
Stir continuously until chips are melted. Pour into a lightly greased
aluminum foil-lined 8"x8" baking pan. Cool. Turn fudge out of pan;
peel off foil. Cut into squares.

Nothing says "cozy home" like the aroma of
fresh-baked gingerbread!

Old-Fashioned Gingerbread   *Makes 10 to 12 servings*

1 c. brown sugar, packed
1 c. molasses
1 c. less 1 T. shortening
2-1/2 c. all-purpose flour
1 t. ground ginger
1 t. ground cloves

1 t. cinnamon
1 c. water
1-1/2 t. baking soda
2 eggs, beaten
Garnish: powdered sugar

Beat together brown sugar, molasses and shortening; set aside. Whisk together flour and spices, then in a separate mixing bowl, combine water and baking soda. Add flour alternately with water to molasses mixture and beat until well combined. Add eggs, stirring well, and pour batter into a greased 13"x9" baking dish. Bake at 350 degrees for 30 to 45 minutes or when cake springs back to the touch. Dust with powdered sugar.

Dress up a dessert tray in no time for a grand
ending to your party! Place Cherry Snowballs in bright
red or gold foil candy cups.

Cherry Snowballs

Makes 3 dozen

1 c. butter, softened
2-1/2 c. powdered sugar, divided
1 T. water
1 t. vanilla extract
2 c. all-purpose flour
1 c. quick-cooking oats,
    uncooked

1/2 t. salt
36 maraschino cherries, drained
1/4 to 1/3 c. milk
2 c. sweetened flaked coconut,
    finely chopped

Blend butter, 1/2 cup powdered sugar, water and vanilla in a large
bowl; set aside. Combine flour, oats and salt; gradually add to butter
mixture. Shape a tablespoonful of dough around each cherry, forming
a ball. Arrange balls 2 inches apart on ungreased baking sheets.
Bake at 350 degrees for 18 to 20 minutes, until golden on bottoms.
Remove to a wire rack to cool. Combine remaining powdered sugar
and enough milk to make a smooth dipping consistency. Dip cookies;
roll in coconut.

Caramel
Chocolate
Pretzels

Dip the ends of pretzel rods in melted chocolate, then
roll in crushed nuts or holiday sprinkles. Package them in
a vintage candy jar for gift-giving!

Chocolate Chip Squares

Makes 2 dozen

1-1/2 c. brown sugar, packed
    and divided
1 c. plus 2 T. all-purpose flour,
    divided
1/2 c. margarine, softened
2 eggs, beaten

2 t. baking powder
1 t. vanilla extract
6-oz. pkg. chocolate chips
1/4 t. salt
1/2 to 1 c. chopped walnuts

Mix together 1/2 cup brown sugar, one cup flour and margarine.
Press into bottom of 13"x9" pan. Bake at 350 degrees for 10 to
15 minutes, or until lightly golden. Mix together remaining
ingredients and pour over hot crust. Bake at 350 degrees for
20 to 25 minutes. When cool, cut into small squares.

Slip a flavored teabag or pressed flower in with your
holiday cards...a sweet surprise!

Hot Cocoa Nog

Makes 4 servings

1 qt. eggnog
3 c. milk
1/2 c. chocolate syrup

1 T. vanilla extract
1/2 t. nutmeg

Combine eggnog, milk and chocolate syrup in a large saucepan over medium heat. Stir constantly until heated through; add vanilla and nutmeg.

Candy cane lane! Glue candy canes, curved side out, around the outside of a clean coffee can for a quick flower vase.

Cinnamon Logs

Makes 4 to 5 dozen

1 c. butter, softened
1 t. almond extract
3 T. sugar

1 T. cinnamon
2 c. all-purpose flour
Garnish: powdered sugar

In a large bowl, blend together butter, almond extract, sugar and cinnamon until light and fluffy. Add flour and beat well. Chill for several hours until dough is firm enough to handle. Using palms of hands, shape teaspoonfuls of dough into one-inch logs. Arrange on ungreased baking sheets; bake at 300 degrees for about 20 minutes, or until golden. Cool on paper towels; sprinkle generously with powdered sugar.

A bowl of red apples and pomanders makes a pretty centerpiece.
Tuck in some greenery sprigs or holly too!

Cranberry-Apple Pudding   *Makes 4 to 5 servings*

4 apples, peeled, cored and
    thinly sliced
1 c. cranberries
1/4 c. raisins

juice and zest of one orange
1/2 t. apple pie spice
1 c. milk
1 c. bread crumbs

Combine all ingredients and place into a 2-quart glass baking dish.
Bake, covered, at 350 degrees for 40 to 50 minutes or until firm in
the center. Serve warm.

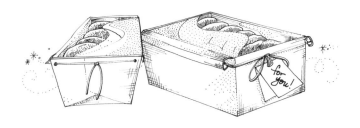

When shipping cookies, place lengths of wax paper between
cookie layers. Add mini marshmallows to make sure
cookies don't move around.

Merry Reindeer Cookies

Makes 2-1/2 dozen

17-1/2 oz. pkg. peanut butter
    cookie mix
1/3 c. oil
1 egg, beaten

60 mini pretzel twists
60 semi-sweet chocolate chips
30 red cinnamon candies

Combine cookie mix, oil and egg in a mixing bowl. Beat until well blended. Shape into a 7-1/2 inch roll; wrap in plastic wrap. Chill for one hour; unwrap and cut into 1/4-inch slices. Place cookies about 2 inches apart on ungreased baking sheets. Using thumb and forefinger, make a slight indentation one-third of the way down the sides of each slice. Press in pretzels for antlers, chocolate chips for eyes and red hots for noses. Bake at 350 degrees for 9 to 11 minutes, or until golden. Remove to wire racks to cool.

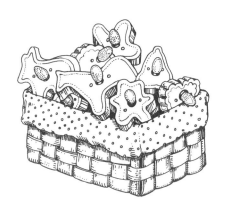

Mini cookie cutters are just the right size to make fudge cut-outs. Pour hot fudge onto wax paper-lined baking sheets and spread to 1/4-inch thickness. Chill until firm and then cut fun shapes with cookie cutters. Remove from wax paper and chill again.

Mrs. Claus's Roll-Out Cookies   *Makes 12 to 14 dozen*

1 T. plus 1 t. baking soda
2 c. sour cream
4 c. butter, softened
4 c. sugar

8 eggs, beaten
2 t. vanilla extract
4 t. baking powder
12 c. all-purpose flour

Dissolve baking soda in sour cream; add butter and sugar. Mix well; stir in eggs and vanilla. Mix in baking powder and flour; roll dough out to 1/4-inch thickness. Cut out with cookie cutters; place on greased and floured baking sheets. Bake at 325 degrees for 8 to 10 minutes; cool. Spread frosting over the top.

Frosting:

2-lb. pkg. powdered sugar
2 c. butter, softened
2 to 4 t. vanilla extract

8-oz. pkg. cream cheese,
  softened
1/4 to 1/2 c. milk

Mix sugar, butter, vanilla and cream cheese together; add enough milk to make desired thickness.

Make cookie giving fun...tuck a variety of wrapped cookies
inside a big Christmas stocking!

Candy Cane Thumbprints

Makes about 3 dozen

2/3 c. butter, softened
1/2 c. sugar
1/4 t. salt
1 egg, beaten

1 t. vanilla extract
1-1/2 c. all-purpose flour
Garnish: finely crushed
    peppermint candies

Blend together butter, sugar and salt with an electric mixer on low speed. Mix in egg and vanilla. Beat in as much flour as possible; stir in remaining flour. Cover; chill for one hour. Shape dough into one-inch balls; place 2 inches apart on ungreased baking sheets. Bake at 375 degrees for 8 to 10 minutes, until lightly golden around edges. Remove from oven; make a thumbprint in each cookie with thumb. Cool. Pipe filling into centers; sprinkle with crushed candy.

Frosting:

1/4 c. butter, softened
1/4 t. peppermint extract

1-1/2 c. powdered sugar
2 to 3 t. milk

Blend together butter and extract. Gradually add powdered sugar and milk to a piping consistency.

Who says glasses should be reserved for beverages?
Elegant stemmed glasses are just right for serving up
desserts like ice cream, pudding and mousse...and it's sure
to make guests feel extra special.

Rich Spice Cake

Makes 8 to 12 servings

2 c. plus 1 T. all-purpose flour, divided
2 t. cinnamon
1 t. ground cloves
1 t. allspice
1/2 t. nutmeg
1 t. baking soda

1 c. less 2 T. milk
2 T. vinegar
1/2 c. shortening
2 c. brown sugar, packed
3 egg yolks, beaten
2 egg whites, stiffly beaten
1 c. raisins

Sift 2 cups flour, cinnamon, cloves, allspice, nutmeg and baking soda together; set aside. Stir milk and vinegar together; set aside. Cream shortening and sugar together in a large mixing bowl; add egg yolks. Gradually mix in flour mixture alternately with milk; fold in egg whites. Toss raisins with remaining flour; fold into batter. Pour into two, 8" round baking pans; bake at 350 degrees for 30 minutes or until toothpick inserted into center removes clean. Cool; frost with your favorite icing.

Gumdrops by the yard! String colorful construction paper circles and gumdrops for a quick & easy garland.

Grandma's Apple Pie

Makes 6 servings

1 c. sugar
3 c. water
1 t. cinnamon
1/8 t. salt
1/4 c. margarine, softened
2 T. cornstarch

8 to 10 apples, peeled, cored
 and sliced
9-inch pie crust
1/4 c. brown sugar, packed
3/4 c. all-purpose flour
2 T. butter

In large saucepan, mix together sugar, water, cinnamon, salt, margarine, cornstarch and apples. Heat on medium high until thickened and apples are soft. Pour apple pie filling into pie crust. Mix together brown sugar, flour and butter with fork until crumbs form. Sprinkle on top of pie filling. Bake at 400 degrees for 15 to 20 minutes.

Did you know...there are 3 towns in the United States
officially named Santa Claus!

Santa's Peanut Butter Fudge   *Makes about 5 dozen*

2/3 c. milk
2 c. sugar
1 c. mini marshmallows

1 c. crunchy peanut butter
1 t. vanilla extract
1/2 c. chopped dates

Combine milk and sugar in a saucepan over medium-high heat.
Bring to a boil without stirring until a candy thermometer registers
240 degrees, or a soft ball forms in cold water. Remove from heat;
add marshmallows, peanut butter, vanilla and dates. Stir just until
combined. Pour into a lightly greased 8"x8" pan; refrigerate at least
20 minutes before cutting.

Wake your family up to Christmas music...what a nice way
to begin the day!

Peppermint Candy Cheesecake   *Makes 12 servings*

1 c. graham cracker crumbs
3/4 c. sugar, divided
6 T. butter, melted and divided
1-1/2 c. sour cream
2 eggs, beaten
1 T. all-purpose flour
2 t. vanilla extract

2 8-oz. pkgs. cream cheese,
   softened
1/4 c. candy canes, coarsely
   crushed
Garnish: frozen whipped
   topping, thawed; crushed
   candy canes

Blend crumbs, 1/4 cup sugar and 1/4 cup melted butter in bottom of
ungreased 8" round springform pan; press evenly over bottom. Blend
sour cream, remaining sugar, eggs, flour and vanilla in a blender or
food processor until smooth. Add cream cheese and blend; stir in
remaining 2 tablespoons melted butter until completely smooth.
Fold in crushed candy and pour over crust. Bake at 325 degrees for
45 minutes. Remove from oven; cool, then refrigerate for 4 hours or
overnight. Loosen pan sides and remove springform; serve garnished
with whipped topping and crushed candy.

Set up a coffee station for friends to enjoy while nibbling on dessert. Make it extra special by offering flavored creamers, candied stirrers and scrumptious toppings like whipped cream, cinnamon and chocolate shavings.

Sugar & Spice Walnuts

Makes 3 cups

1 c. sugar
1/4 t. salt
1/2 to 1 t. cinnamon

6 T. milk
2-1/2 c. walnuts
1 t. vanilla extract

Combine sugar, salt, cinnamon and milk in large saucepan. Cook over medium-high heat, stirring constantly until the mixture reaches the soft ball stage, about 234 to 240 degrees on a candy thermometer. Remove from heat, add walnuts and vanilla. Mix well until nuts are coated and spread in a single layer on a sheet of wax paper to cool.

Oh! the snow, the beautiful snow, filling the sky and earth below.

–J.W. Watson

Chocolate Chip Macaroon Bars

Makes 2 dozen

1/2 c. butter
1 c. plus 2 T. all-purpose flour,
 divided
1-1/2 c. brown sugar, packed
 and divided
2 eggs, beaten

1/4 t. salt
1 c. chopped pecans
1-1/2 c. sweetened flaked
 coconut
1 t. vanilla extract
1 c. semi-sweet chocolate chips

Mix together butter, one cup flour and 1/2 cup brown sugar. Pat into the bottom of a 13"x9" greased baking pan. Bake at 325 degrees for 15 minutes. In medium bowl, blend together remaining flour and brown sugar, eggs, salt, pecans, coconut, vanilla and chocolate chips. Spread mixture onto baked crust. Bake for an additional 25 minutes. Cut into bars when cool.

Package your homemade goodies...fudge, peanut brittle or spiced nuts, in airtight containers, then slip them in gift bags tied with raffia. Set several in a basket by the door so there will always be a treat waiting for guests to take home.

Cinnamon Almonds

Makes 4 cups

1 egg white	1/2 c. sugar
1 t. cold water	1/4 t. salt
4 c. whole almonds	1/2 t. cinnamon

Lightly beat egg white; add water and beat until frothy but not stiff.
Add almonds; stir until well coated. Mix sugar, salt and cinnamon in
a small bowl. Sprinkle over almonds, toss to coat and spread evenly
on a lightly greased baking sheet. Bake for one hour at 250 degrees,
stirring occasionally, until golden. Cool; store in an airtight container.

INDEX

APPETIZERS

Cherry Tomato Appetizers	13
Christmas Cheddar Wafers	9
Christmas Puffs	17
Festive Holiday Spread	15
Holiday Cheese Ball	3
Mini Ham Puffs	11
Parmesan-Bacon Dip	7
Parmesan Crostini	21
Sweet Pumpkin Dip	5
Wintry Snack Mix	19

BEVERAGES

Apple-Cinnamon Punch	27
Christmas Wassail	23
Hot Cocoa Nog	101
Mama's Warm Spiced Milk	29
Peppermint Eggnog Punch	25

BREADS

Eggnog Bread	37
Poppy Seed Bread	33
Quick Holiday Loaf	35
Rosebud Dinner Rolls	31

COOKIES & CANDY

Candy Cane Thumbprints	111
Cherry Snowballs	97
Chocolate Chip Macaroon Bars	123
Chocolate Chip Squares	99
Cinnamon Almonds	125
Cinnamon Logs	103
Merry Reindeer Cookies	107
Mrs. Claus's Roll-Out Cookies	109
Peppermint Snowballs	89
Santa's Peanut Butter Fudge	117
Snowy Day Fudge	93
Sugar & Spice Walnuts	121

DESSERTS

Baked Cinnamon Pudding	91
Cranberry-Apple Pudding	105
Date-Nut-Cherry Fruitcake	39
Grandma's Apple Pie	115
Old-Fashioned Gingerbread	95
Peppermint Candy Cheesecake	119
Rich Spice Cake	113
Triple Chocolate Bundt® Cake	87

INDEX

MAINS

3-Cheese Shells Florentine	85
Busy-Day Lasagna	83
Christmas Eve Pot Roast	65
Cider-Baked Ham	79
Cranberry-Glazed Pork Roast	77
Easy Elegant Turkey	71
Holiday Roast Turkey	73
Italian Stuffed Chicken	81
Maple-Glazed Turkey Breast	69
Perfect Prime Rib Roast	67
Whole Baked Ham	75

SIDES

Apple-Mallow Yam Bake	45
Cheddar Potatoes	51
Cheesy Scalloped Corn	57
Cornbread Stuffing	41
Creamed Peas & Onions	53
Crockery Sage Dressing	43
Garlic Mashed Potatoes	49
Herbed Rice Pilaf	63
Old-Fashioned Corn Pudding	59
Savory Spinach	55
Spiced Fruit	61
Sweet Potato Casserole	47

Our Story

Back in 1984, we were next-door neighbors raising our families in the little town of Delaware, Ohio. Two moms with small children, we were looking for a way to do what we loved and stay home with the kids too. We had always shared a love of home cooking and making memories with family & friends and so, after many a conversation over the backyard fence, **Gooseberry Patch** was born.

We put together our first catalog at our kitchen tables, enlisting the help of our loved ones wherever we could. From that very first mailing, we found an immediate connection with many of our customers and it wasn't long before we began receiving letters, photos and recipes from these new friends. In 1992, we put together our very first cookbook, compiled from hundreds of these recipes and, the rest, as they say, is history.

Hard to believe it's been over 25 years since those kitchen-table days! From that original little **Gooseberry Patch** family, we've grown to include an amazing group of creative folks who love cooking, decorating and creating as much as we do. Today, we're best known for our homestyle, family-friendly cookbooks, now recognized as national bestsellers.

One thing's for sure, we couldn't have done it without our friends all across the country. Each year, we're honored to turn thousands of your recipes into our collectible cookbooks. Our hope is that each book captures the stories and heart of all of you who have shared with us. Whether you've been with us since the beginning or are just discovering us, welcome to the **Gooseberry Patch** family!

Visit our website anytime
www.gooseberrypatch.com

Jo Ann & Vickie

1·800·854·6673